W9-BGN-784

DRAW FANTASY

DRAGONS, CENTAURS & OTHER MYTHOLOGICAL CHARACTERS

By Shari Cohen

Illustrated by Frank Dixon

LOWELL HOUSE JUVENILE

LOS ANGELES

CONTEMPORARY BOOKS

CHICAGO

Copyright © 1997 by RGA Publishing Group, Inc.
All rights reserved. No part of this work may be reproduced or transmitted in any form or
by any means, electronic or mechanical, including photocopying and recording, or by any information
storage or retrieval system, except as may be expressly permitted by the 1976 Copyright Act or
in writing by the publisher.

President and Publisher: Jack Artenstein
Director of Publishing Services: Rena Copperman
Executive Managing Editor, Juvenile: Brenda Pope-Ostrow
Editor in Chief, Juvenile: Amy Downing
Editor: Jessica Oifer
Cover and Interior Design: Lisa-Theresa Lenthall
Typesetter: Carolyn Wendt

Lowell House books can be purchased at special discounts when ordered in bulk for premiums and
special sales. Contact Department TC at the following address:

Lowell House Juvenile
2020 Avenue of the Stars, Suite 300
Los Angeles, CA 90067

Library of Congress Catalog Card Number: 97-21763

ISBN: 1-56565-770-5

Manufactured in the United States of America

10 9 8 7 6 5 4 3 2 1

CONTENTS

INTRODUCTION

Draw Fantasy: Dragons, Centaurs & Other Mythological Characters takes you on a magical journey into the world of myth, folklore, and legend. Characters from Greek, Roman, and Norse mythology, as well as other fantastical figures, come to life on the pages of this unique drawing book.

You will not only learn to draw every character, but you'll experience the frustration and anger of the giant Cyclops, feel the Fenrir wolf's fury, and comprehend the hypnotizing beauty of the goddess Venus. You'll meet a powerful yet kind dragon who was held captive under the water for over two thousand years, and marvel at the amazing deeds of the Roman hero Hercules. On page 64, you'll even find a chart listing the equivalent Greek and Roman gods.

So gather your paper, pencil, and an eraser and get ready to let your imagination soar. You are about to travel into a wondrous world of myth, mystery, and magic.

DRAWING TIPS

Want to make your drawing the best that it can be? Before you begin creating your mythological masterpieces, read through the following tips that every aspiring young artist should know.

- Use a large sheet of paper and make your drawing fill up the space. That way, it's easy to see what you are doing, and it will give you plenty of room to add details.

- When you are blocking in large shapes, draw by moving your whole arm, not just your fingers or your wrist.

- Experiment with different kinds of lines: do a light line, then gradually bear down for a wider, darker one. You'll find that just by changing the thickness of a line, your whole picture will look different! Also, try groups of lines, drawing them straight, crossing, curved, or jagged.

- Remember that every artist has his or her own style. That's why the pictures you draw won't look exactly like the ones in the book. Instead, they'll reflect your own creative touch.

- Most of all, have fun!

WHAT YOU'LL NEED

PAPER

Many kinds of paper can be used for drawing, but some are better than others. For pencil drawing, avoid newsprint or soft papers because they don't erase well. Instead, use a large pad of bond paper (or a similar type). The paper doesn't have to be thick, but it should be uncoated, smooth, and cold pressed. You can find bond paper at an art store. If you are using ink, a dull-finished, coated paper works well. Textured, colored paper works best with charcoal.

PENCILS, CHARCOAL, AND PENS

A regular school pencil is fine for the drawings in this book, but try to use one with a soft lead. Pencils with soft lead are labeled #2; #3 pencils have a harder lead. If you want a softer or thicker lead, ask an art store clerk or your art teacher for an artist's drafting pencil.

Charcoal works well when you want a very black line, so if you're just starting to draw with charcoal, use a charcoal pencil of medium to hard grade. With it, you'll be able to rub in shadows, then erase certain areas to make highlights. Work with large pieces of paper, as charcoal is difficult to control in small drawings. And remember that charcoal smudges easily!

If you want a smooth, thin ink line, try a rolling-point or a fiber-point pen. Art stores and bigger stationery stores have them in a variety of line widths and fun, bright colors.

If you are drawing on colored paper, you may want to experiment with a white pastel pencil. It creates bright highlights when combined with a black pen or a charcoal pencil.

ERASERS

An eraser is one of your most important tools! Besides removing unwanted lines and cleaning up smudges, erasers can be used to make highlights and textures. Get a soft plastic type (the white ones are good), or for very small areas, a gray kneaded eraser can be helpful. Don't take off ink with an eraser because it will ruin the drawing paper. If you must take an ink line out of your picture, use liquid whiteout.

OTHER HANDY TOOLS

Facial tissues are helpful for creating soft shadows—just go over your pencil marks with a tissue, gently rubbing the area you want smoothed out.

A square of metal window screen is another tool that can be used to make shadows. Hold it just above your paper and rub a soft pencil lead across it. Then rub the shavings from the pencil onto the paper to make a smooth, shadowed area in your picture. If you like, you can sharpen the edge of the shadow with your eraser.

You will also need a pencil sharpener, but if you don't have one, rub a small piece of sandpaper against the side of your pencil to keep the point sharp.

FINISHING YOUR DRAWING

As you'll see with the fascinating figures in this book, artists must use different drawing techniques to distinguish between the various body parts and make the characters look real. Here are some useful techniques for giving your drawings a natural look.

HATCHING

Hatching is a group of short, straight lines used to create a texture or a shadow. The hatching can either show that the surface is flat, using straight lines, or how rounded it is, depending upon the amount of curve in the lines. This technique is handy when texturing a character's curved body parts or the folds in a garment. When you draw the hatching lines closer together, you create a dark shadow. For a very light shading, draw the lines shorter, thinner, and farther apart. Notice how hatching lines are used to draw the rough fur on the Fenrir wolf's body.

CROSS-HATCHING

This technique gives your figure a wrinkled or textured look. Start with an area of hatching, then crisscross it with a new set of lines. If you are drawing wrinkles on the skin, make the lines a bit wobbly and uneven, just as creases in real skin would be.

Look at this drawing of King Arthur. The cross-hatching makes his armor and shield look as if they are made of chain-link metal, which was often used to make armor during the time period in which King Arthur lived.

STIPPLE

When you want to give your drawing a different feel, try the stipple technique. All you need are dots! This method works best with pen, because, unlike a pencil, a pen will make an even black dot by just touching the paper.

The stipple technique, used in this drawing of Medusa, is very similar to the way photos are printed in newspapers and books. If you look through a magnifying glass at a picture in the newspaper, you will see very tiny dots. The smaller and farther apart the dots are, the lighter the area is. The larger and closer the dots are, the darker the area. In your drawings, you can make a shadow almost black just by placing your stipple dots closer together.

SMOOTH TONE

By using the side of your pencil, you can create a smooth texture on your figure. Starting with the areas you want to be light, stroke the paper very lightly and evenly. Put a little bit more pressure on your pencil as you move to the areas you want to be darker. If you want an area even smoother, go back and rub the pencil with a facial tissue, but rub gently! If you get smudges in areas you want to stay white, simply remove them with an eraser. Try using this smooth texture on Venus's long, flowing dress.

Now that you're armed with the basic drawing tools and techniques, you're ready to get started on the figures in this book. What's more, you'll learn fascinating facts as you draw.

At the back of the book are extra techniques and hints for using color and scale to make the most of your drawings.

THE LOATHSOME DRAGON

Stories of fire-breathing dragons vary throughout different cultures. The English fairy tale "The Loathsome Dragon" tells of the kind Princess Margaret, who is transformed into a hideous dragon by her evil stepmother, the queen.

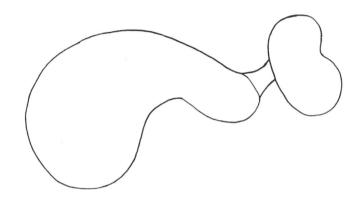

1 *Draw the beginning shapes for the dragon's head, neck, and body.*
After the spell is cast, the dragon Margaret flees to the secluded countryside. Day after day, month after month, she sits under a tree, waiting for her brother, Childe Wynd, to return from his journeys at sea and rescue her from the evil curse.

2 *Refine the head shape, and insert the shapes for three of the four legs. Then add the tail and the outline of the wing.*
During this time, the pitiful tale of the curse of the Loathsome Dragon—as the people call Margaret—travels throughout the neighboring ports and villages. When Childe Wynd hears of his sister's fate, he immediately sets sail for home.

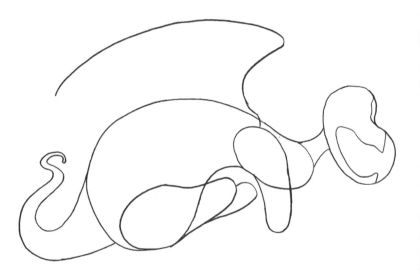

3 *Further refine the body, wings, and head. Draw eyes and ears, and add the outline of the dragon's fourth leg, as well as all the outlines for its feet. Erase unneeded lines.*
But the wicked queen casts another spell—stirring up the ocean waters to prevent Childe Wynd from landing his ship at home. Each time Childe Wynd brings his boat close to shore, fierce winds and huge waves push him back.

4 *Define the legs, feet, and back of the head. Insert the teeth and the second wing. Erase more unneeded lines.*

When he finally reaches shore, Childe Wynd searches everywhere until he at last finds himself face-to-face with the dragon. He cannot believe this hideous monster is his sister. He draws his sword to slay the beast. But when he hears the dragon's sweet familiar voice, he realizes that it is truly his sister, Margaret.

5 *Add details, including the dragon's facial features and sharp claws. Add guidelines for the dragon's scales, and begin to insert some of the scales. Draw spines on the dragon's back, and further detail its wings.*

Childe Wynd approaches the dragon and gently kisses the top of its head. Magically, the spell is broken. With a hiss and a moan, the Loathsome Dragon collapses to the ground, and Princess Margaret emerges.

6 *Draw the rest of the scales on the dragon's body. Add any remaining details, then shade.*

The brother and sister then rush off to the queen's castle, where they pluck a magic twig from a nearby bush. They toss the twig at their wicked stepmother and cast their own spell on her. The queen shrieks in horror, shrivels into a hideous toad, and hops down the castle steps in dismay.

9

THE UNICORN

The unicorn is a mystical animal that is found in the mythologies of many different cultures throughout the world. Representing beauty, goodness, and strength, this legendary creature appears in art, folklore, and literature.

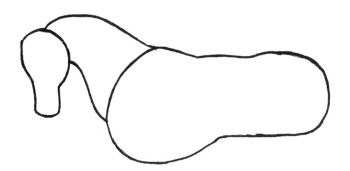

1 *Draw the main shapes for the head, neck, and body.*
The unicorn resembles a white horse, but it has a long spiral horn protruding from the middle of its forehead. This horn is said to have the magical power to heal, create, and destroy.

2 *Add the ears, horn, and upper legs.*
The unicorn has its roots in several ancient cultures. In China, it is called K'i-lin (kee-LEEN), and this gentle creature represents good fortune and long life. In Japan, the unicorn is known as the Kirin (kee-REEN). It has the ability to identify one who is guilty of a crime. The Kirin fixes its eyes upon a guilty person and then pierces that person through the heart with its horn.

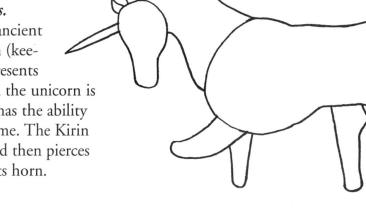

3 *Sketch the eye and the nose. Draw the shapes for the unicorn's mane and tail, as well as its lower legs. Begin to shape its hindquarter.*
To the people of the Middle Ages (especially during the fifteenth century), the unicorn was a symbol of love and purity. During that period, images of the white beast appeared in churches, paintings, books, and even in the wood carvings of doorways.

Refine the overall body shape, then add definition to the face, horn, mane, hooves, and tail. Erase any unneeded lines.

Europeans of the Middle Ages believed in the magical power of the unicorn's horn. They believed that drinking from the horn could cure illness and infection. Small shavings from the horn were even used for medicinal purposes. Doctors carried powders that supposedly contained horn shavings from the unicorn.

5

Add the unicorn's final details, which include hatching and shading.

After the fifteenth century, interest in the unicorn diminished. But it began to blossom again in the nineteenth century. In fact, in his story *Through the Looking Glass,* Lewis Carroll writes about a chance meeting between his protagonist, Alice, and the unicorn. They look at each other in amazement, two creatures from different worlds, and both promise to believe in each other's existence from that moment on.

THE AZURE DRAGON

There are many different types of dragons in Chinese mythology. Most of them are known to be both generous and wise. Some represent good luck. The Azure Dragon is the most powerful Chinese dragon. A spiritual dragon, he controls the weather.

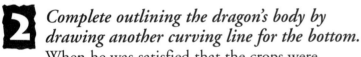

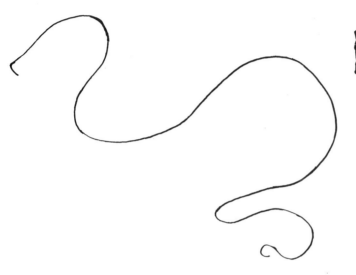

1 *Draw the curving line for the top of the dragon's body.*
Chien Tang, as this Azure Dragon was called, lived deep inside a well in a small village in China. Chien Tang's duty was to fly up to the clouds and bring rain down upon the earth so that crops could grow.

2 *Complete outlining the dragon's body by drawing another curving line for the bottom.*
When he was satisfied that the crops were flourishing, Chien Tang returned to his well and lived quietly until the earth needed watering again. The people were grateful to Chien Tang. They wrote him poems and messages of gratitude and dropped them into his well.

3 *Add the shapes for the eyes, mouth, wings, and legs.*
One day a strange man wandered into the village. He watched the people drop gifts down to Chien Tang. How silly to waste lavish gifts on a dragon, he thought. The man began to taunt and ridicule Chien Tang.

4 *Begin to refine the shapes of the wings and the legs, and create circular outlines for the claws. Add details to the eyes, mouth, and snout. Erase unneeded lines.*

Chien Tang grew furious. He flew up into the sky and created a giant rainstorm. For years, rain poured down upon the village. Crops were ruined, and the people lived in misery. Finally, the Supreme Ruler of Heaven threw Chien Tang into the lake and bound the dragon to a pillar inside the dragon king's palace at the bottom of the lake.

5 *Insert the first layer of feathers on the wings. Add another line to the dragon's underbelly, and further refine the legs and tail. Draw the shapes for the claws, and continue to detail the dragon's face and head.*

Chien Tang remained at the bottom of the lake for 2,000 years. During this time, the dragon king's beautiful daughter was given in marriage to the cruel river dragon. He greatly mistreated the princess and forced her to work like a peasant.

6 *Further refine the dragon's face, adding the teeth and the second whisker. Refine the claws, legs, and tail. Add more feathers to the wings, as well as to the dragon's back and head. Insert lines for scales on the dragon's underbelly. Erase unneeded lines.*

One day a young man named Liu came by the river and noticed the beautiful girl hard at work. The two began to talk, and the princess told Liu of her mistreatment. She asked him to take a letter to her father.

13

7 Complete the feathers on the dragon's wings and body. Add a tongue to the dragon's mouth. Further define the claws, and continue adding scale lines to the dragon's body.

When the dragon king received the letter, he read it out loud. He wept as he learned of his daughter's plight. Moments later, a roar as loud as a hundred thunderstorms came from the bottom of the lake. Then Chien Tang rose to the surface. With the pillar still chained to his back, he flew off to rescue the princess.

8 Draw the rest of the scales on the dragon's body. Refine all shapes, then shade.

Chien Tang swallowed the evil river dragon in one gulp, and then went to beg the Supreme Ruler's forgiveness for his behavior 2,000 years ago. The ruler released Chien Tang from the pillar, and the heroic dragon returned the princess to her father. Chien Tang then flew off to once again control the rain.

THE CHINESE DRAGONS

There are four kinds of Chinese dragons. Celestial dragons rule the heavens and live high in the Palace of the Gods. Spiritual dragons control the wind and the rain and can be seen flying through the clouds. Earth dragons inhabit the land, overseeing the rivers and streams. The underground dragons live beneath the earth, guarding precious metals and treasures.

CADMUS AND
THE THREE-HEADED SERPENT

According to Greek mythology, the hero Cadmus slew the three-headed serpent. From the serpent's teeth—which he buried in the ground—sprang mighty warriors who helped Cadmus build the city of Thebes, in Greece.

1 *Draw the main shapes for Cadmus's head and body, as well as for the serpent's three heads.*
One day, Cadmus was summoned by the oracle at Delphi, a divine spirit who could see into the future. The oracle told Cadmus that it was his destiny to found a great new city. He instructed Cadmus to follow a cow that he would find outside the oracle's temple. On the spot where the cow laid down, he said, the city should be built.

2 *Draw the outlines for Cadmus's upper legs and arms. Insert the curving line for the underside of the serpent's body.*
Cadmus and his men followed the cow for hours over the hills and through valleys. At last the cow laid down next to a group of trees. This was the spot where Cadmus would build his city.

3 *Add the shapes for Cadmus's lower legs and arms. Draw the other side of the serpent's curving body, then begin to outline its three mouths.*
As they stood on this spot, Cadmus and his men heard the gurgling sounds of a nearby spring. Cadmus sent his men to fetch some water. They took their jugs and went off to the spring. Near the spring there was a cave hidden by some branches.

4 *Add circles for Cadmus's hands and feet, and begin to refine his arms and legs. Add curving lines for the serpent's topmost neck, and continue to detail its facial features. Erase unneeded lines.*

Suddenly, a hideous serpent head with a long, sharp black tongue jutted out of the cave's entrance. Moments later, a second head popped out of the cave, and then a third. Finally, a single body emerged to completely reveal a three-headed serpent.

5 *Define Cadmus's hands and feet. Complete the serpent's tail, and insert its middle neck and fangs.*

The three-headed serpent struck out at the men with all three of its sharp, poisonous tongues. After being touched by a tongue, one of Cadmus's men fell dead. The serpent killed one man after another, then crushed their lifeless bodies with its great strength.

6 *Continue to refine Cadmus, then sketch his shield and spear. Begin to draw lines on the serpent's body. Erase any unneeded lines.*

Meanwhile, Cadmus became worried. He could no longer hear his men, and so he made his way toward the spring. There, he saw all of his men lying dead on the ground. Then Cadmus saw the serpent, which lunged at him.

7 *Complete Cadmus's spear, and further detail his body. Add more lines to the serpent's body and head, and insert its three tongues.*

But before its poisonous tongue touched him, Cadmus drew his spear and plunged it deep into the evil monster's belly, killing it.

8 *Add the remaining details to Cadmus and his shield. Finish drawing the lines on the serpent's body. Further define its tongues.*

Then Cadmus heard the voice of the goddess Athena (the Roman goddess Minerva). She told him to pull out all of the serpent's teeth and plant them in the earth. She said hundreds of armed warriors would spring like trees from the ground. And that is precisely what happened.

9 *Complete the drawing by shading.*

To stop the warriors from turning on him, Cadmus threw a stone at them. The warriors began to attack one another— unsure of who had thrown the stone—until only five of them were left. These five strong men joined Cadmus and helped him build the city of Thebes. Cadmus became the great city's first king.

THE TROLL

According to Scandinavian folklore, trolls are hostile creatures who live inside dark caves in the mountains. They are keepers of buried treasures such as silver and gold, and are known for their pointed ears, long noses, and large teeth.

 Draw shapes for the troll's head, body, and upper arms and legs.
Most trolls cannot tolerate sunlight. If exposed to even the smallest amount, a troll may burst into tiny pieces or turn to stone. While trolls remain hidden during the day, they spend their nights hunting elves—their favorite food—and prowling nearby villages for treasures.

 Insert the beginning shapes for the troll's eyes, eyebrows, and mouth. Draw circular outlines for its lower left arm, as well as its hands and feet.
The Scandinavian story "The Trolls of Dovrafell" tells about a pack of unruly trolls who come down from the mountains every Christmas Eve to wreak havoc on the tiny home of a man named Halvor.

 Begin to refine the shape of the troll's head, hands, feet, and body. Add more detail to its face, and insert its ears. Erase unneeded lines.
Some of these trolls are quite large, bigger than Halvor himself. But the smaller trolls always do the worst damage, smashing furniture and throwing food from the cupboards. They tear down curtains, bang pots and pans, and screech wildly.

18

4 *Further refine the troll's face, hands, feet, and body. Add in its bowl and spoon. Erase more unneeded lines.*
One Christmas Eve, Halvor and his family are visited by a hunter and his gentle white bear. When the trolls invade Halvor's home as usual, they tease the white bear, poking sharply at its nose and jumping up and down on top of it.

5 *Draw the troll's teeth and toenails, as well as a band around its right foot. Further detail its face, and add liquid to its bowl. Begin to draw fur all over the troll's body.*
Soon the white bear loses its patience. Its eyes grow dark with fury, and it lets out a deep growl. Its growl grows into a roar so loud, it shakes the tiny house. The bear then lunges forward, and the pack of trolls runs from the house and back up to the mountains.

6 *Add more fur to the troll's head and body, then shade.*
The following Christmas Eve, Halvor is chopping wood when he hears a voice call out to him. "Halvor, do you still have your big white cat?" it asks, mistaking the white bear for a cat. "I do," he answers. "She has seven kittens and each is bigger and meaner than she." "You'll never see us anymore," the voice squeals. And sure enough, Halvor never does.

POWERS OF THE TROLLS

According to legend, trolls can live to be 500 years old. In fact, it is almost impossible to kill a troll because it has the ability to regenerate, or regrow, a lost or severed body part in a matter of days. This ability makes trolls excellent warriors.

THE JINNI

A jinni (JEE-nee) is a spirit from Arab and Muslim folklore that inhabits the earth and can assume human or animal form. Jinn (plural for jinni) have many supernatural powers, such as the ability to cast spells on people and grant them wishes.

1 *Draw the main shape for the jinni's head, then sketch the curving line for its body. Insert the small oval for its lamp.*

According to Arab mythology, jinn are powerful creatures that came down to earth from the heavens before humankind existed. They made their homes in rocks and trees, underneath the earth, and in fire.

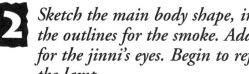

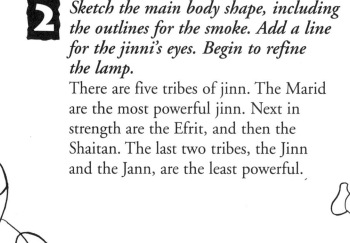

2 *Sketch the main body shape, including the outlines for the smoke. Add a line for the jinni's eyes. Begin to refine the lamp.*

There are five tribes of jinn. The Marid are the most powerful jinn. Next in strength are the Efrit, and then the Shaitan. The last two tribes, the Jinn and the Jann, are the least powerful.

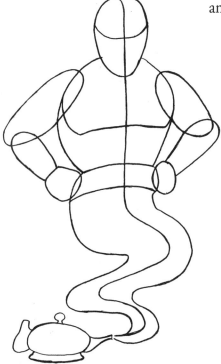

3 *Add the outlines for the arms and hands, and begin to detail the jinni's body. Further refine the lamp.*

Because a jinni is a spirit, it can look human, but it cannot be caught and bound. Jinn cannot be burned either. One might even suddenly appear in the flame of a hot fire. Some jinn can change their shapes, turning themselves into animals and other objects by just a wink of an eye or the snap of a finger.

4 *Draw a curved line for the jinni's hair, and add the beginning shapes for the facial features. Refine the body, arms, hands, and lamp.*

While a jinni might play tricks on unsuspecting humans, a human can summon and control a jinni if he or she knows the correct magic word or gesture. Once a jinni is summoned, the human can make that jinni do whatever he or she wants.

5 *Finish refining the jinni and its lamp, and further detail its face and chest. Erase any unneeded lines.*

Those people living during the pre-Islam period were both fascinated and mystified by the jinni's amazing powers. Because people thought the jinni was able to predict the future, fortune-tellers often used messages from them in their own predictions.

6 *Insert finishing details, then shade. Place a shadow under the lamp.*

Because of its mischievous ways and magical powers, the jinni is a favorite subject of many stories throughout the world. The most popular story is *A Thousand and One Nights* from Arab folklore. In this story, one jinni inhabits an old battered oil lamp. A young man named Aladdin rubs the lamp three times, and the jinni appears and grants him three wishes.

21

KING ARTHUR

King Arthur ruled Great Britain during the sixth century, a time of continual war. Though he was a real man and a great king, amazing legends about his magical power and strength are known throughout the world.

1 *Draw the main shapes for the head and body.*
Arthur was born the son of King Uther Pendragon of Britain. Immediately after Arthur's birth, the king gave Arthur to Merlin, the court magician, because he feared for his baby's life during this time of constant war. Merlin took Arthur to a kind man named Sir Hector, who raised Arthur as his own son.

2 *Add the oval shapes for the legs and the one visible arm.*
Arthur's life was fairly normal until he reached the age of fifteen, when a large stone suddenly appeared outside a local church. There was a sword stuck in the stone. Men from all over the land tried to pull the sword out of the stone, but they failed.

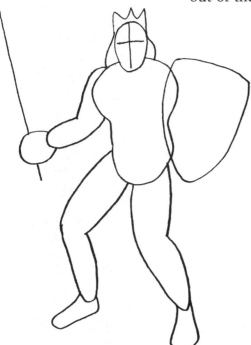

3 *Insert the guidelines for the facial features. Add the outlines for the hair and the crown, as well as for the feet and the hand. Draw the beginning shape for the shield, then start the sword.*
Then young Arthur approached the wedged sword. He leaned forward and easily pulled the sword from the stone. The townspeople gasped in amazement as Arthur held the sword high for all to see. The sword, called Excalibur, would provide Arthur with many years of victory and glory in battle.

4 *Add the facial features, and begin to refine the body, hand, and sword. Sketch the outlines of Arthur's armor, then put in the beginning shapes for the designs on his armor and shield.*

Around this time, Arthur's father, King Pendragon, died, and the people of Britain needed a new king to protect them from the cruelty of the Saxon invaders. Young Arthur became that new king.

 5 *Draw the rest of the facial features, and refine Arthur's armor and shield. Erase any unneeded lines.*

Although he was admired by many, King Arthur had some enemies. During a vicious battle in southwest England, one of his biggest enemies, Mordred, attacked Arthur. Defending himself, Arthur killed Mordred but was mortally wounded himself.

 6 *Add finishing details, then shade. Use cross-hatching to create the woven metal texture of the armor and shield.*

In a sad and haunting ceremony, the king was carried away by angels on a magic barge to the mysterious island of Avalon, in order to be healed back to life. According to legend, one day Arthur will return once again to reign as the king of England.

THE KNIGHTS OF THE ROUND TABLE

After each successful battle, King Arthur and his knights met around a large round table and told stories about their conquests. These men soon became known as the Knights of the Round Table. Why a round table? King Arthur considered all of his knights equal to himself. To prove this, the king sat with them at a round table where there was no head.

THE CYCLOPS

The Cyclops is a giant monster from Greek mythology that has one eye in the middle of its forehead. One of the most well-known Cyclopes is Polyphemus, son of the sea god Poseidon.

 1 *Draw the main shapes for the head, body, arms, and upper legs.*
Polyphemus lived in a remote cave high in the mountains of Sicily, Italy, where he spent his days tending his flock of goats. One day a ship carrying Odysseus, the king of the small Greek island Ithaca, arrived at Sicily. Odysseus and his men left their ship to explore the land and wandered into Polyphemus's cave.

2 *Add the lower legs and the club, as well as the long eyebrow and the mouth.*
Making themselves comfortable, the men lit a fire, ate cheese, drank, laughed, and talked. Suddenly, they heard a thunderous noise. Polyphemus had entered his cave, enraged to find these strange men enjoying his food and drink. He placed a giant rock to block the cave's entrance.

3 *Add the ears and the facial features. Refine the overall body shape, the club, and the boots. Erase any unneeded lines.*
Polyphemus grabbed two of the men and devoured them. Then he seized another man, and another. Odysseus's men sat paralyzed with fear as they watched their companions being eaten, one by one.

Further detail the Cyclops, including its eye, teeth, and clothes.
Finally, Odysseus came up with a plan to save the remaining crew. He gave Polyphemus a drink of wine from a bowl. The giant liked the wine and called out for more. Again and again, Odysseus filled the bowl until Polyphemus fell asleep. Then Odysseus took a long, sharpened wooden stake and plunged it deep into the sleeping giant's eye.

 Refine the Cyclops and the club, and darken the eye and the mouth.
Blinded, the enraged Polyphemus stumbled around the cave in search of the men. But Odysseus and his men quickly tied themselves to the bellies of Polyphemus's goats and were safely hidden from the giant. Eventually, Polyphemus opened the cave's entrance to let out his herd, and the men escaped, right under the giant's nose.

 **Complete your drawing, shading where needed.**
When they reached the safety of their boat, the men called out mockingly to Polyphemus. Realizing he had been tricked, he hurled a giant boulder toward the ship. The boulder just missed the ship, and the lucky men set out to sea.

THE FATE OF ODYSSEUS

Once Odysseus and his men escaped from the terrifying Cyclops, their troubles were not over. The revengeful Polyphemus yelled to his father, the sea god Poseidon, to punish Odysseus and his men. "Grant that Odysseus may never come close to his home in Ithaca!" he bellowed. Poseidon heard his son's cry and stirred up the seas with ravaging storms and tidal waves. It took Odysseus and his men ten years to finally make it home to Ithaca— though most of the men died while at sea.

ODIN

Odin is the chief god in Norse mythology. This tall bearded one-eyed god lives in Asgard—the Norse heaven—where he observes the entire world with the help of his two ravens, Huginn and Muninn.

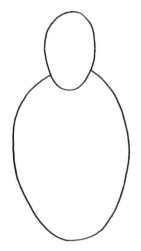

1 *Begin by drawing circular shapes for the head and the body.*
Each morning, Odin sends his ravens to fly out over the world and observe the day's happenings. At noon, the ravens return and whisper all they have learned in Odin's ear. Odin then uses that information, along with his great wisdom, to establish laws governing the entire universe.

2 *Add the shapes for the legs and the arms.*
Odin gained much of his great wisdom at the cost of one of his eyes. According to legend, one day Odin encountered the wise and gentle giant Mimir, the guardian of the magic Well of Wisdom. Mimir had gained his own wisdom by drinking water from the well each morning.

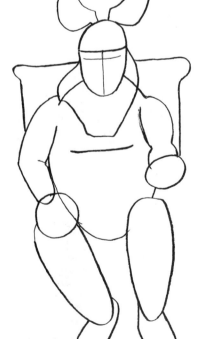

3 *Insert the shapes for Odin's beard, hat, hands, and feet. Begin to refine the arms, and insert the guidelines for the facial features. Then draw the back of Odin's throne. Erase unneeded lines.*
Odin asked Mimir if he could have a drink from the well. The giant agreed, but only if Odin surrendered one eye—through which the giant would be able to observe any place in the world. Odin consented, gave Mimir his right eye, and then drank from the well.

4 *Refine and add hands, facial features, and wings on the hat. Draw a line for the spear, and complete the outline of the throne. Erase any unneeded lines.*

Odin was also a brave and powerful fighter. He carried a spear called Gungnir, which never missed its target when Odin threw it. He rode a magical horse called Sleipnir, which had eight legs and took Odin through the air and over the seas.

5 *Further refine Odin's body, face, clothes, and throne. Add the point to the spear. Erase any unneeded lines.*

One of Odin's greatest enemies was the frost giant Ymir. Ymir was powerful and evil tempered. Odin knew that there would be no peace until the giant was gone forever. Therefore, the chief god and his brothers, Vili and Ve, planned a surprise attack and killed the wicked giant.

6 *Add remaining details, shading where indicated.*

From Ymir's dead body, Odin created the earth, called Midgard. He cut deep valleys and high mountains from Ymir's body, and he made walls to surround the earth from the giant's eyebrows. Then Odin helped the other gods create man from an ash tree and woman from an elm tree.

THE NORSE WORLDS

In Norse mythology there are four distinct worlds: that of the giants, the gods, the humans, and the underworld. The giants and the gods are the most powerful beings and are constantly warring with one another. The giants inhabit the world of Jotunheim, and the gods live in the heavens, called Asgard. Humans live on earth, or Midgard, which was created from the giant Ymir's body. The underworld, known as Niflheim, is the home of the dead.

VENUS

Venus, the Roman goddess of love and nature, had neither a mother nor a father. Rather, she sprang full-grown out of the ocean waters on a cushion of foam. She floated upon the gentle waves and was so beautiful that the wind almost lost its breath.

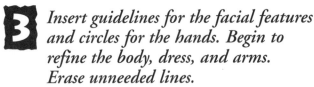

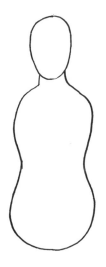

1 *Draw the main shapes for the head, neck, and upper body.*
After Venus sprang to life, the wind blew soft, gentle gusts and guided her to the island of Cyprus. There, she was welcomed by three maidens who dressed her in dazzling garments and sparkling jewels.

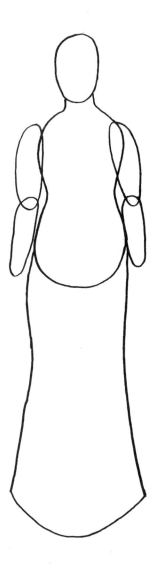

2 *Add the oval arm shapes, as well as the outline for Venus's dress.*
Venus was then placed in a chariot drawn by white doves and led to the home of the gods. The gods placed her on a golden throne and made her a goddess.

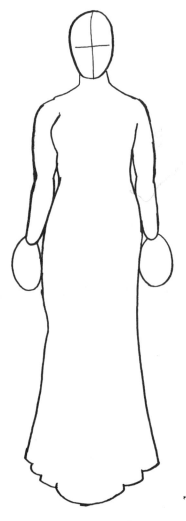

3 *Insert guidelines for the facial features and circles for the hands. Begin to refine the body, dress, and arms. Erase unneeded lines.*
Venus was adored by everyone—humans and gods alike. Even Jupiter, the king of the gods, wanted the beautiful goddess as his wife. But Venus rejected him. To punish her, Jupiter gave Venus in marriage to his son Vulcan, a skilled craftsman but a rather dim-witted and ugly god of fire.

4 *Draw the beginning shapes for the eyes, nose, and mouth. Define the hands, and begin to detail the dress. Erase any more unneeded lines.*

Vulcan could not believe his luck. He immediately fell in love with Venus. He built her a beautiful palace and made the most lavish jewels for her. He even wove her a golden girdle containing a magic spell that made the goddess much more beautiful.

5 *Refine the facial features and dress. Add hair, and further define the hands.*
The goddess of love was not at all pleased with being the wife of the solemn, hardworking Vulcan. She soon fell in love with Mars, the handsome god of war. She left Vulcan to be with Mars, and the two had a son—the mischievous little boy named Cupid, who became the winged god of love.

6 *Add finishing details, including the texture on the hair. Shade Venus using smooth tones where needed.*
Venus and Mars remained together for a while, but the beautiful goddess of love soon tired of him. She went on to have numerous love relationships with various gods and humans.

THE WEREWOLF

Of all the world's monsters, the werewolf is one of the most well-known and most feared. According to legend, a werewolf is a human being who actually transforms into a ferocious wolf at night.

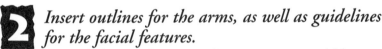

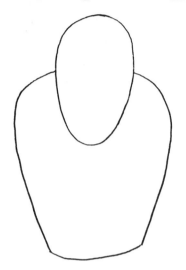

1 *Draw the shapes for the werewolf's head and body.*
During the Middle Ages (fifth to fifteenth centuries), people feared the wolf, believing it to be one of the most vicious animals alive. It was during this time that stories of people who transformed into hairy creatures that devoured humans first began to surface throughout Europe.

2 *Insert outlines for the arms, as well as guidelines for the facial features.*
It was believed that an ordinary person could become a werewolf if he or she became possessed by an evil, demon spirit. Strangely, some humans actually tried to transform themselves into these powerful beasts. They did this by rubbing a magical ointment on their bodies while chanting a magical spell, or by dressing in a garment made from the skin of a wolf.

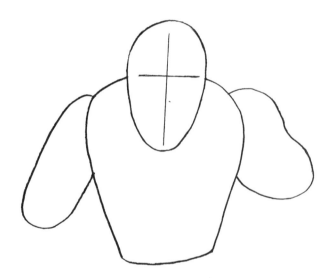

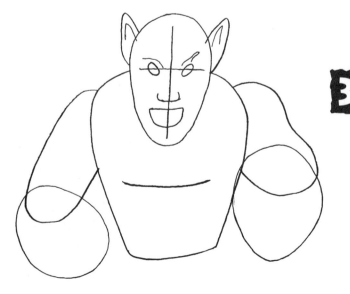

3 *Add outlines for the eyes, eyebrows, nose, mouth, and ears. Insert circles for the hands, and add a chest line.*
The complete transformation into a wolf took place in a matter of minutes. The human features such as the nose and the mouth disappeared and were replaced by a long snout. Fur grew all over the body, and the person sprouted a short bushy tail.

Refine the facial features, hands, and upper body. Begin putting hair on the face. Erase any unneeded lines.
The creature then prowled throughout the night, devouring both people and animals. When the sun came up, the werewolf returned to its human form.

Add details, including the werewolf's teeth, shirt, and claws. Thicken the facial hair.
While in their human form, werewolves were said to have straight furry eyebrows that met on the bridge of the nose. They also had curved fingernails and a long hairy middle finger on each hand.

Insert hair all over the werewolf's body and head. Finish by using hatching to shade.
Anyone who had bad scratches or bruises on his or her skin was also under suspicion of being a werewolf. It was thought that such injuries might have been received while running through the woods while hunting at night.

MEDUSA

In Roman and Greek mythology, Medusa is one of three terrible Gorgon sisters. She has snakes in her hair and bronze claws on her hands. Anyone who looks directly at Medusa immediately turns to stone.

1 *Begin by drawing the outline of Medusa's head, and the bodies of three snakes.*

Medusa began her life as a beautiful human, admired for her long, flowing hair. When the sea god Neptune (the Greek god Poseidon) began to fall in love with her, the goddess Minerva (the Greek goddess Athena) became jealous and changed Medusa into a hideous Gorgon, a creature with a head full of snakes.

2 *Insert guidelines for her facial features. Draw the bodies of the remaining four snakes.*

Years later, Minerva completed her destruction of Medusa when she helped the young hero Perseus slay the hideous Gorgon. In order to save his mother, Perseus was ordered—by Polydectes, the cruel king of the island Seriphos—to kill and behead Medusa. Minerva helped him by giving him her shield as protection.

3 *Draw Medusa's eyes, as well as lines for her nose and mouth. Sketch her neckline.*

After days of traveling, Perseus finally spotted Medusa. To avoid being turned to stone, Perseus looked at the monster through her reflection in Minerva's shield. As he moved nearer, he grew more and more horrified by her repulsive appearance.

4 *Refine Medusa's facial features, and add her eyebrows. Draw the eyes and mouths on the snakes. Erase the guidelines on Medusa's face.*

With one sweep of his sword, Perseus severed Medusa's head from her body. He then quickly stuffed her head inside his sack. Moments later, Perseus watched as the beautiful winged horse Pegasus sprang from the monster's severed neck.

5 *Further refine Medusa's facial features. Add the snakes' teeth, and insert the lines on their bodies. Erase more unneeded lines.*

The young hero then took flight for the island of Seriphos in the winged sandals given to him by the god Dis (the Greek god Hades).

6 *Add finishing details, then shade using stippling.*

When Perseus arrived on Seriphos, he rescued his mother from Polydectes by turning him to stone with Medusa's still deadly head. He then gave the head to the goddess Minerva, who attached the head to her shield to help her in future battles.

APOLLO

A pollo is the god of music, poetry, and the sun. The most handsome and most beloved of all the gods in Greek mythology, Apollo is the son of the god Zeus and the goddess Leto. He drives a golden chariot led by white swans across the skies, and he shoots a bow with golden arrows.

1 Draw the shapes for the head and body.
Of Apollo's many loves, one of the best known is Daphne, the beautiful daughter of the river god Peneus. Apollo pursued Daphne persistently, but she had no interest in him. She vowed never to marry and would not even listen to the exquisite sound of Apollo's harp.

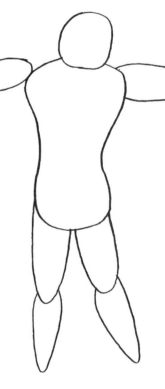

2 Add the oval shapes for the arms and legs.
One afternoon, Apollo approached Daphne to tell her again how much he loved her. When she ran from him, Apollo followed, begging her to stop and listen. Daphne would not stop. She sped swiftly across the meadow toward the bank of her father's river.

3 Insert circular shapes for the hands and feet. Form the beginning shape for the bow.
Daphne called out to her father to save her. But Peneus could not rise out of the riverbed quickly enough to rescue his daughter. He put another plan into action.

4 *Refine the hands and feet, as well as the bow. Add the hairline, the visible eye, and the outlines of Apollo's clothing.*

As Daphne's toes touched the sand of the riverbank, a strange sensation came over her. Her body felt numb and her feet became rooted in the earth. Tree bark surrounded her body. Her arms changed into branches and her head transformed into a treetop. Before Apollo could do anything, Daphne was turned into a laurel tree.

5 *Add more facial features and the arrow. Refine the clothing and the body, including the hands and feet. Erase any unneeded lines.*

As he neared the tree, Apollo could hear the beating of Daphne's frightened heart inside the bark. He promised her that her tree would be eternally green. Taking laurel from the top, he made a wreath with its shimmering leaves.

6 *Add finishing details, then shade using smooth textures.*

The laurel wreath became the prize awarded in later athletic and musical competitions. It also became Apollo's symbol. The god has been depicted in sculptures and paintings wearing the crown of laurel on his head.

THE FIRST OLYMPIC GAMES

One of Apollo's earliest heroic deeds was the slaying of the serpent Python, a deadly monster that lived in a cave near the city of Delphi. When the people of Delphi prayed to Apollo to save them from the horrible beast, Apollo came down from Mount Olympus, the home of the gods, and killed the serpent with one of his golden arrows. In honor of this victory, Apollo started the Pythian games. Chariot and footraces were held every four years in Greece. These competitions are similar to the Olympic games of today.

THOR

Thor is the Norse god of thunder and the sky. Large and strong, he protects humans and gods against evil forces. Thor lives in a region of heaven called Thrudvangar. Thursday (Thor's day) is named for him.

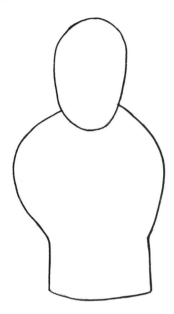

1 *Draw the beginning shapes for Thor's head and body.*
Thor had a fierce temper and was thought to be the best fighter and the strongest of the Norse gods. He had a bristling red beard and glowing eyes. Nicknamed "the thunderer," Thor's huge form and booming voice terrified his enemies.

2 *Add circles for his upper arms, as well as lines for his hat and belt.*
Thor carried an indestructible weapon—a hammer that produced lightning bolts and returned to his hand after he threw it. He wore an iron glove to protect his hand from the heat of the hammer. Thor also had a magic belt that, when buckled around him, doubled his strength.

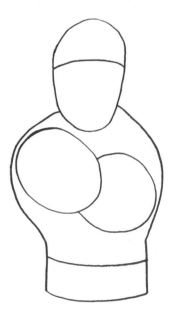

3 *Insert the outlines for his lower arm and hand. Add details to his hat and belt, and put in his eyes and nose.*
Thor's greatest enemies were the devious frost giants and the trolls. The two groups hardly gave Thor a moment of peace, constantly playing tricks on him in order to get him mad.

4 *Form Thor's mouth, beard, and eyebrows. Then add details, including his iron glove, his hammer, his belt end, and the horns on his hat.*

One morning, Thor awoke to find a frost giant named Thrym had stolen his hammer. To get it back, Thor disguised himself as the beautiful goddess Freya. Thrym wanted to marry Freya, and so Thor thought disguising himself as her, and pretending to be Thrym's bride, was a good way to get near him.

5 *Refine drawing, and sketch Thor's long, flowing beard and hair. Erase any unneeded lines.*

Thor wore Freya's golden necklace, her clothes, and a wedding veil. He went to Thrym's palace with the god Loki, who disguised himself as Freya's maid. Thrym displayed a delicious banquet of food for the wedding.

6 *Add remaining details, including his lightning bolt, then shade.*

Thrym watched his "bride" gobble up a whole roasted steer, eight salmon, and three platters of meat. He then lifted the veil to kiss Freya, only to see Thor's flaming red beard and glowing eyes. Thrym raised Thor's hammer to throw it at the god, but Thor lunged forward, grabbed the hammer, and struck down the giant.

THE FROST GIANTS

According to Norse mythology, long before the earth was formed, there existed two worlds: a dark, cold world called Niflheim and a hot, fiery world called Muspell. Eventually, sparks from the fire of Muspell, along with heat and steam, drifted into the cold mist of Niflheim. The collision of hot and cold produced a blast of frost from which emerged the evil frost giant named Ymir. From Ymir sprang an entire race of frost giants who were ill-tempered and at constant war with the Norse gods. When Ymir was killed by Odin, the blood from his wounds drowned all the frost giants except Bergelmir, who escaped with his family to continue the race of frost giants.

HYDRA

The nine-headed serpent Hydra is one of the most hideous and ghastly monsters of Greek mythology. Until it was slayed by Heracles, Hydra was almost indestructible because two crude heads would spring up to replace each head that a slayer would sever.

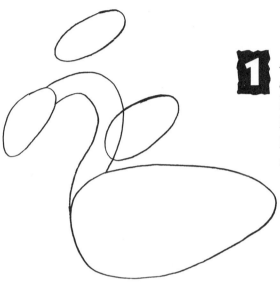

1 *Draw the main body shape, as well as three heads and the neck.*

Hydra was the child of the terrible monster Typhon, who had 100 heads and 200 evil eyes that oozed venom. Hydra lurked in the steamy swamps near the city of Lerna, in Greece, feeding on the flesh and blood of nearby cattle.

2 *Insert the remaining six heads and three more necks.*

The beast contained so much poison that the fumes from its breath were enough to kill whatever came close to it. Each of Hydra's heads was grotesque and deadly, but the center head was the most dangerous, as it was immortal.

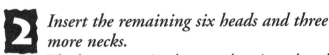

3 *Draw the rest of Hydra's necks, and add the beginning shapes for its three visible legs.*

For years, warriors made futile attempts to destroy this horrible creature. Then, one day, the beast was defeated by Heracles (Hercules in Roman mythology), one of the strongest heroes of Greek mythology.

4 Begin to shape each of Hydra's nine heads. Then add circular outlines for its feet.

To atone for a past crime against his own family, Heracles was put under the control of his cousin, King Eurystheus (you-RIS-thee-us), who hated Heracles. Eurystheus sent Heracles to perform twelve difficult labors, which included battles against monsters, giants, animals, and even gods.

5 Refine the shapes of the heads, legs, feet, and body. Add ears, eyes, and a tail. Erase any unneeded lines.

The second of Heracles's twelve labors was to slaughter Hydra. Armed with clubs, swords, and arrows, and accompanied by his companion Iolaus (eye-YO-lay-us), Heracles approached the deadly Hydra and began to attack.

6 Add claws, teeth, and lines on the tail. Also add lines on some of the necks to outline an area for the front scales.

He filled his enormous lungs with air, held his breath—so as not to inhale Hydra's poison—and ran at the creature. Heracles then used his clubs to knock off Hydra's heads, one after another. Each head hit the ground with a thud and rolled to the side.

7 *Draw scales on the fronts of Hydra's necks. Insert more lines on the tail, and add detail to the eyes and snouts.*

But no sooner had Heracles knocked off one head than two new ones grew in its place. In desperation, Iolaus set the neighboring woods on fire to try to burn Hydra to death—but Hydra survived!

8 *Add finishing details and shade. Draw shadows where indicated.*

Then Heracles came up with another idea. He dipped his sword in the hot flames and burned the flesh of each of Hydra's necks so that no new heads could grow. With Iolaus's help, he then buried the immortal center head under a huge rock. He returned to Eurystheus, victorious from his battle with Hydra.

ALTERNATE APPENDAGES

Hydra's ability to grow two heads when one was cut off can be compared with the habits of the octopus. After an attack by one of its enemies, an octopus can regrow lost arms, or tentacles, and sometimes a tentacle end may branch into two or more arms. This is called regeneration.

THE CHIMERA

The Chimera is a huge fire-breathing monster that has the head of a lion, the body of a dragon, and the hind legs of a goat. According to Greek mythology, the Chimera ravaged the Greek city of Lycia until it was slayed by the prince of Corinth, Bellerophon (buh-LAIR-uh-fuhn).

 1 *Draw the beginning shapes for the head and body.*

The people of Lycia were terrified of this immense beast. It captured and killed everyone in its path with its deadly fire-breath. In fact, the fire that came from its mouth was so hot, it blackened and scorched the hills and valleys around the city.

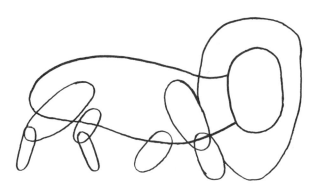

 **2** *Insert oval shapes for the outlines of the mane and legs.*

During this time, the handsome prince of Corinth—Bellerophon—was visiting the nearby city of Argos and committed a crime of improper conduct against the king of Argos's wife. Despite this crime, the prince was well loved by the people of Argos, and so the king sent him to King Iobates of Lycia for punishment rather than punishing the prince himself.

 3 *Refine the legs, then add the shapes for the ears, feet, tail, and front wing. Draw guidelines for the facial features. Erase any unneeded lines.*

King Iobates, however, did not want to take responsibility for harming Bellerophon either. Instead, he sent the prince out on a heroic, but almost impossible, task—to kill the ferocious Chimera. The king felt confident that Bellerophon would never return alive.

4 *Continue to refine the body shape and the feet. Add the eyes, mouth, and back wing. Erase any more unneeded lines.*

Bellerophon did not fear his punishment. He had always enjoyed a challenge and was pleased at the thought of such a great adventure. But he knew that in order to conquer the Chimera, he needed the help of the great white-winged horse Pegasus.

5 *Further refine, then add details. Include the nose, lines on the front wing, scales on the tail, claws on the front feet, and hooves on the back feet. Erase unneeded lines.*

When Bellerophon spotted the horse drinking from a nearby pond, he quietly approached it and gently asked for its help. Pegasus knelt down, and Bellerophon placed a bridle over the horse's head. Then the two rode up through the clouds in search of the Chimera.

6 *Add more detail to the face, including sharp fangs. Insert the guidelines for the scales on the body.*

Just as the sun began to set, they spotted the monster standing on a pile of jagged rocks. When it saw Bellerophon and Pegasus approaching from above, it jumped and kicked, hissed and roared, as its long, slithery tail snapped against the stones.

7 *Complete the scale guidelines with crisscrossing lines, then begin to insert some of the scales. Add more detail to the face, mane, and wings.*

Pegasus swooped down toward the Chimera while Bellerophon fitted an arrow to his bow. Bellerophon then readied his aim and shot the arrow deep into the monster's side. Next, he stuffed lead into the weakened Chimera's mouth. The lead melted from the Chimera's fiery breath and trickled down inside the creature's body, where it hardened and killed the beast.

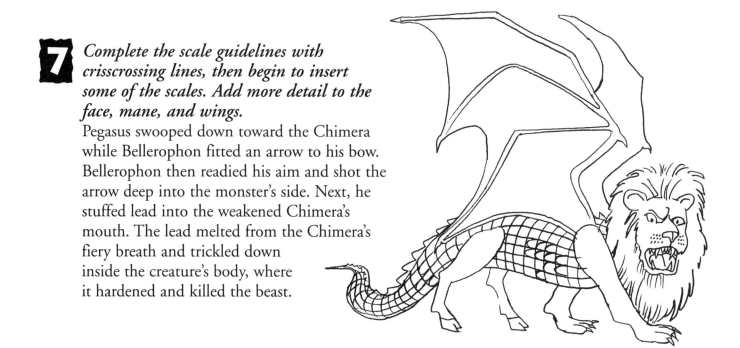

8 *Finish the Chimera's scales and mane. Shade the drawing using smooth tones.*
Bellerophon returned victorious to King Iobates. Free for the first time from the threat of the Chimera, the people of Lycia were relieved. The king forgave the prince his crimes and offered Bellerophon his daughter's hand in marriage.

43

QUETZALCOATL

Quetzalcoatl (ket-suhl-kuh-WAH-tuhl) is the legendary god who ruled the Toltec and later the Aztec people in ancient Mexico. Known as the "feathered" or "plumed serpent," Quetzalcoatl appeared in two forms—as a snake covered with colorful features and as a light-skinned bearded man.

1 *Draw the outline of the feathered serpent's head, as well as the curved line for its body.*

Quetzalcoatl was a god of purity and goodness. He controlled the rising and setting of the sun, and he even had the power to bring the dead back to life. He would often visit the underworld, called Mictlan, to bring deceased humans back to earth.

2 *Complete the outline of the body, then insert the mouth.*

He was also a humble god who did not think himself above difficult manual labor. He worked side by side with his people, teaching them how to farm, polish gemstones, and weave fabrics.

3 *Draw guidelines for the feathers on the serpent's body. Add the eyes and the fangs.*

Quetzalcoatl's enemy was Tezcatlipoca, god of the night sky. Tezcatlipoca ruled in another part of the Toltec region. He had little compassion for living things and enjoyed hurting humans. Tezcatlipoca despised Quetzalcoatl because of the love and respect the serpent god showed his people.

 4 *Add crisscrossing lines to the feather guides. Add details to the eyes, and insert the teeth.*

One day Tezcatlipoca disguised himself as a feeble old man and approached Quetzalcoatl. He held a mirror in front of his enemy's face. Quetzalcoatl suddenly realized how old and worn he was—he had always thought of himself as eternally young and handsome. He threw the mirror down in dismay.

 5 *Complete the crisscrossing guidelines, and begin to draw feathers on the serpent's head and body. Add a nose and a tongue, and further refine the facial features.*

The old man smiled and offered Quetzalcoatl a potion to calm him. Quetzalcoatl drank much of the potion and became so drunk, he could not perform his duties. Tezcatlipoca then seized control of Quetzalcoatl's people.

 6 *Add detail to Quetzalcoatl's tongue. Draw the rest of the feathers and shade.*

The evil god exiled Quetzalcoatl from his city. The serpent god wandered the desert for days, weeping over the loss of his beloved city. When he finally came to the ocean shore, he wove a raft and sailed off into the sunset.

THE RETURN OF THE KING

Before Quetzalcoatl set sail, he swore to his people that one day he would return to them. He would arrive in a ship that would come from the sunrise. To this day, there are Mexicans who gather to watch the sunrise and wait for the return of their leader, Quetzalcoatl.

JORMUNGAND, THE MIDGARD SERPENT

According to Norse legend, Jormungand, the Midgard serpent, was tossed into the depths of the ocean by the god Odin, who had a premonition that the serpent would one day bring disaster to the world.

1 *Draw the curving line for the top of the serpent's body.*
Living in the sea, Jormungand grew so huge, it could wrap its entire body around the earth. For this reason it was known as the Midgard serpent—Midgard is the Norse name for earth.

2 *Insert another curving line to complete the bottom of the serpent, except where its body will be covered by water.*
Jormungand had exceptional vision as well as the ability to change shapes and regenerate, or regrow, lost or severed body parts. It also could spit a poison so deadly, it could destroy even the powerful Norse gods.

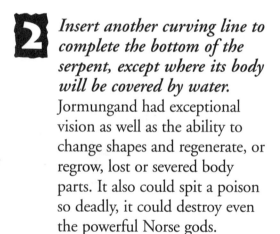

3 *Add the mouth and the visible eye. Insert curved lines around the bottom of the serpent's body to show the water's surface.*
Like the frost giants, the Midgard serpent was an enemy of the Norse gods. When the frost giant Utgard-Loki asked Jormungand to help him trick the Norse god Thor, the Midgard serpent readily agreed.

 4 *Add the serpent's teeth and nostril, as well as the spines along its back. Erase unneeded lines.*

Jormungand disguised itself as Utgard-Loki's pet cat. Then Utgard-Loki challenged Thor—who prided himself on his strength—to lift the cat up from the ground. Thor struggled with all his might to lift the cat, but the cat would not budge.

5 *Further detail the serpent's face. Add the curved line to show the shape of the earth. Insert lines detailing the water and the continents.*

After several attempts, Thor grew extremely frustrated and gave up. Then the cat transformed back into the Midgard serpent. When Thor realized he had been tricked, he became furious.

 6 *Add finishing details to the serpent and the background. Shade the serpent using stippling.*

According to Norse legend, this is not the last encounter between Jormungand and Thor. They will meet again for a final battle, when the Midgard serpent will come out of the sea and fight with Thor. Thor will strike down the serpent with his indestructible hammer. But before it dies, Jormungand will spit its poison on Thor and kill him.

WHEN THE END COMES

In Norse mythology, Ragnarok is known as the final battle. It is the time when all the forces of evil will rise up against the Norse gods of Asgard. The Midgard serpent will rise out of the sea and spit poison all over the land. The giant Fenrir wolf will break free from its binding chains, and the frost giants will attack the gods. During this time, the earth will sink into the ocean, the sun will turn black, and most of the Norse gods will die.

THE CENTAUR

In Greek mythology, the centaurs are a group of monsters that live in the mountains near the city of Arcadia in Greece. From the waist up, their bodies are human, and their lower bodies and legs are in the form of a horse.

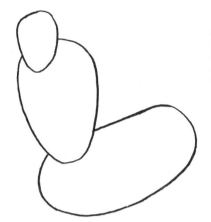

1 *Begin by drawing the circular outlines for the head and the body.*

The centaurs lived without regard to order. They did not honor the gods, nor did they respect humans and their laws. They galloped down from the mountains, trampling and destroying fields and crops and causing trouble wherever they went.

2 *Add the outlines for the upper arms and legs, and begin to refine the lower back.*

One centaur, however, was different from all the others. The son of the Greek god Cronus, Chiron was an immortal centaur known for his kindness and wisdom.

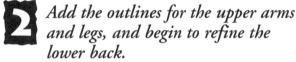

3 *Form the shapes for the lower arms and legs. Continue to refine the lower back. Erase any unneeded lines.*

In fact, Chiron was considered the greatest teacher of courage and knowledge throughout Greece. Both kings and gods brought their small sons to Chiron so that he could raise them with the strength and dignity of heroes.

Refine the arms and legs, and add circles for the hands and feet. Insert guidelines for the facial features and chest.

Two of the greatest Greek heroes—Jason and Achilles—were raised by Chiron. Jason grew to be physically strong and skilled in all sports, and Achilles became one of the greatest Greek warriors.

 Define the hands, body, and feet. Add the eyes and the nose. Erase any unneeded lines.

Even the god Apollo brought his son Asclepius to Chiron. The wise centaur taught Asclepius about medicine and how to heal the ill. Under Chiron's guidance, Asclepius became the first trained physician.

Refine the overall body shape, and insert the tail. Add the mouth, eyebrows, and the centaur's club. Erase any more unneeded lines.

Sadly, Chiron's good deeds came to an end when he was accidentally wounded by Heracles. The Greek hero went to visit his friend Pholus, a centaur who lived near Chiron. Heracles and Pholus opened a bottle of wine, and the aroma of the wine floated through the air, attracting all the centaurs in the area.

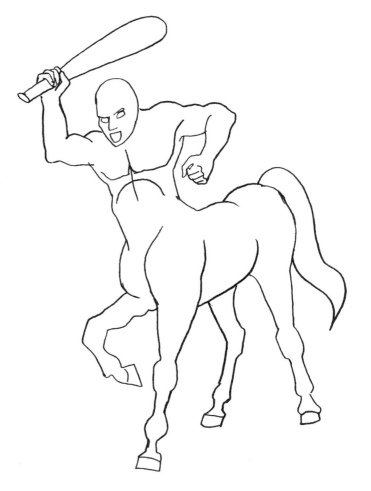

49

7 *Begin adding details, including muscle definition and hair on the head, legs, and body.*

The centaurs came charging toward Heracles in search of the wine. Heracles was able to fight them off, but he accidentally wounded Chiron, who had not taken part in the attack but happened to be nearby.

8 *Add finishing details, then shade using hatching and cross-hatching.*

Because Chiron was immortal, he could not die. However, Chiron's wounds were severe and painful. Zeus, the chief Greek god, therefore allowed the kind centaur to die rather than live forever in pain.

HOUSES OF HEALING

According to Greek mythology, Asclepius's success as a doctor continued to grow after Chiron's death. People worshiped him as a god and even built temples in his honor. Asclepius placed beds inside the temples, which served as the first Greek hospitals.

AGNI

The red-skinned Hindu fire god Agni has three heads and five arms. He flies swiftly through the air, surrounded by a circle of hot flames.

1 *Draw the shapes for Agni's three heads and body.*
Mischievous in nature, Agni delights in startling unsuspecting humans by igniting small fires. Yet, despite his tendency to pull pranks, Agni loves and respects humans. He is kind, honest, and known to turn his destructive firepower against evil spirits and demons.

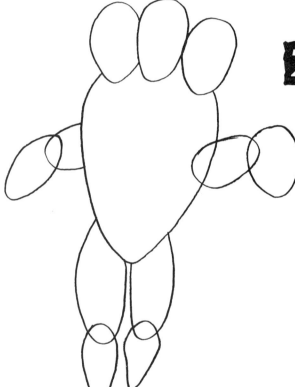

2 *Add outlines for the legs and two of the arms. (Only four of his arms will show.)*
There was a time when Agni was banished from the earth by the powerful Hindu leader Bhrgu. One day, Bhrgu was away from his home when Puloman, an evil being, arrived at his door. Not realizing who the strange visitor was, Bhrgu's wife, Pulomaa—who was pregnant—invited him to sit near the fire.

3 *Refine the shape of the legs, and insert outlines for the other two visible arms and the stomach.*
When she turned her back, Puloman leaned forward into the fire pit and asked the fire god Agni if Pulomaa was the wife of Bhrgu. The demon was once going to marry a woman named Pulomaa, but she married Bhrgu instead. Puloman wondered if this was the same woman.

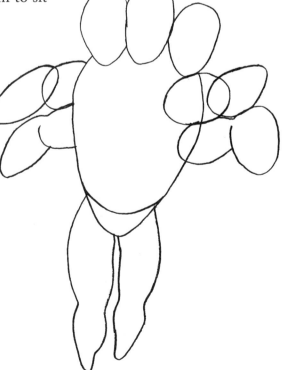

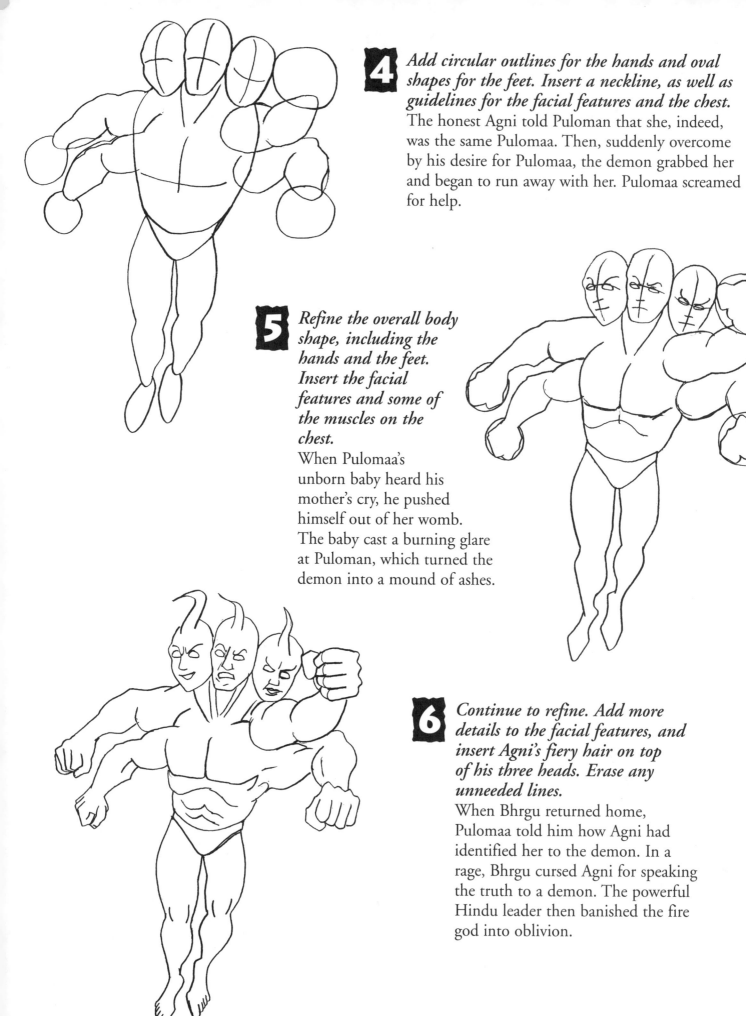

4 *Add circular outlines for the hands and oval shapes for the feet. Insert a neckline, as well as guidelines for the facial features and the chest.*
The honest Agni told Puloman that she, indeed, was the same Pulomaa. Then, suddenly overcome by his desire for Pulomaa, the demon grabbed her and began to run away with her. Pulomaa screamed for help.

5 *Refine the overall body shape, including the hands and the feet. Insert the facial features and some of the muscles on the chest.*
When Pulomaa's unborn baby heard his mother's cry, he pushed himself out of her womb. The baby cast a burning glare at Puloman, which turned the demon into a mound of ashes.

6 *Continue to refine. Add more details to the facial features, and insert Agni's fiery hair on top of his three heads. Erase any unneeded lines.*
When Bhrgu returned home, Pulomaa told him how Agni had identified her to the demon. In a rage, Bhrgu cursed Agni for speaking the truth to a demon. The powerful Hindu leader then banished the fire god into oblivion.

7 Draw more muscles, and further refine the facial expressions. Add fingernails to Agni's hands.

Agni's absence was immediately felt throughout the world. Candles could not be lit, lamps were not able to burn, and hearths lay barren. Desperate, the people called upon Brahma, their god of creation, to restore their god of fire and light.

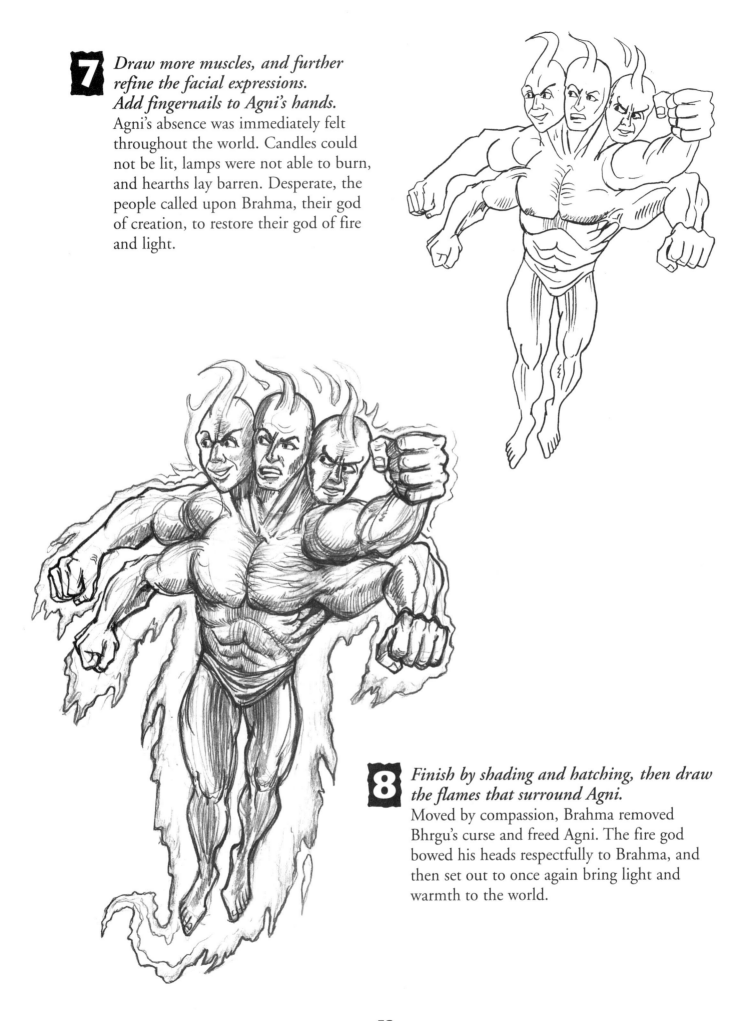

8 Finish by shading and hatching, then draw the flames that surround Agni.

Moved by compassion, Brahma removed Bhrgu's curse and freed Agni. The fire god bowed his heads respectfully to Brahma, and then set out to once again bring light and warmth to the world.

53

FENRIR

Fenrir is a large ferocious wolf with fierce yellow eyes and a tremendous jaw. When it was just a pup, the Norse gods captured it and locked it in a cage because they feared the wolf might one day be responsible for the destruction of the world.

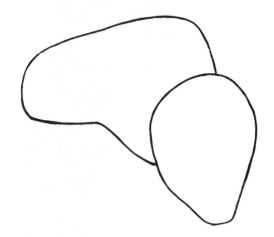

 1 *Draw the main shapes for the head and the body.*
As the young wolf grew, it became even more savage. To keep the world safe from it, the gods decided to trick Fenrir and bind it in a heavy iron chain. To test the chain's strength, the gods challenged Fenrir to show its own strength and try to break out of the chain.

 2 *Insert the outlines for the legs and the feet and a line for the tail. Begin to refine the shape of the head.*
The wolf accepted the challenge and broke the chain with ease. The gods quickly made a heavier chain, but Fenrir broke out of that one as well. The gods then asked the gnomes—tiny magical creatures who lived in the forest—to create an indestructible magic bond to restrain the beast.

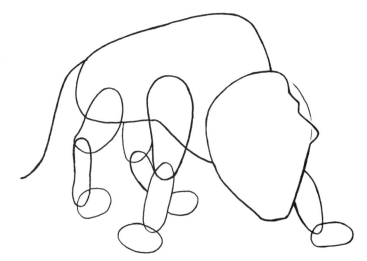

 3 *Refine the legs and the feet, and complete the tail. Add the ears and the mouth. Erase any unneeded lines.*
The gnomes created a magic ribbon named Gleipnir. Again, the gods had to trick the wolf into being bound. This time, they told Fenrir its strength and courage would be doubled if it broke through the unique bond.

 Continue to refine the overall body shape and the mouth. Insert the wolf's sharp claws and fangs, as well as its eyes.

Fenrir suspected that the gods were trying to trap it. Therefore, the wolf asked one of the gods to place a hand in between its jaws while it was bound. Fenrir felt the gods would not trick it if one of them was in danger of being hurt.

5 Add details to the face, including the rest of the teeth, the nostrils, the pupils, and the tongue. Put fur all over the body.

The gods then bound Fenrir with the magic ribbon, and one of them placed his hand in Fenrir's mouth. The wolf tried and tried to break free, but it could not. It flew into a frustrated rage, clamped down hard with its jaws, and bit off the brave god's hand.

6 Complete the fur, then add shading where needed.

The gods quickly placed a sword inside the wolf's mouth to prevent it from biting down again. Then they tied the wolf to a boulder one mile down into the earth, and they placed an even larger boulder on top. Finally, Fenrir was detained.

THE MINOTAUR

The Minotaur is a Greek monster—with the head of a bull and the body of a man—that feasts on human flesh. It roamed freely about the tiny villages on the island of Crete in Greece.

1 *Draw the shapes for the head, body, and upper arms and legs.* The people of Crete were so afraid of the Minotaur, they rarely left their homes. Finally, the ruler of Crete, King Minos, ordered a group of men to capture the savage monster.

2 *Insert the outlines of the lower arms and legs, then sketch the horns.* The king then summoned the skilled craftsman Daedalus to construct a maze, or labyrinth, underneath the palace to house the Minotaur once it was captured. Daedalus designed a maze of paths and passageways so confusing, the fearful monster would never get free.

3 *Begin to refine the body, arms, and legs. Draw circular shapes for the hands and feet, as well as the line for the top of the snout. Erase any unneeded lines.* To keep the beast fed, King Minos invaded the city of Athens. He vowed to destroy the city unless he was sent seven maidens and seven young men every year for nine years as sacrifices, or food, for the Minotaur.

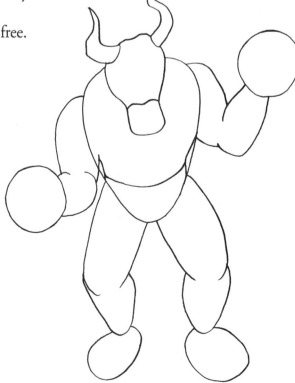

4 *Refine the hands and feet. Add the ears, eyes, mouth, nostrils, and some of the muscles on the chest. Erase any more unneeded lines.*

When the young Athenian hero Theseus heard about these cruel deaths, he volunteered to be one of the beast's victims. He hoped to slay the monster once inside the labyrinth, putting an end to these unnecessary sacrifices.

 5 *Add more head and body details, including the many muscles.*

Just before Theseus entered the labyrinth, King Minos's daughter, Ariadne—who had fallen in love with Theseus—gave the hero a magic ball of thread that unraveled as he walked through the maze. Ariadne held tightly to the other end so that after Theseus slayed the Minotaur, he could follow the thread and find his way out.

 6 *Complete the belt and other finishing details, then shade.*

Theseus found the Minotaur lying asleep at the center of the labyrinth. He snuck up on the beast and killed it with his bare hands. Then he quickly found the other victims who were wandering through the maze, and with the help of the magic thread, he led them safely out.

57

BRINGING YOUR CHARACTER TO LIFE

Here are tips on how to put life into your drawings. Keep in mind that the most realistic drawings combine several finishing techniques. You can practice and experiment with your favorite combinations.

CAST SHADOWS

The simplest thing you can do to make your drawing look rounded and real is to give it a shadow. To do this, you must imagine where the shadow of your character's form would be if it were resting on a flat surface with light coming from above. When light is shining down on Quetzalcoatl from its right, the feathered serpent casts a shadow that extends out to its left side. Notice how the shadow can appear on the underside of a figure, as shown here, as well as on the ground next to it. When creating shadows, make them thinner under narrow body parts and thicker under fuller body parts.

LIGHT FIGURE, DARK BACKGROUND

You'll be surprised how rounded your character will look if you simply darken the space behind it. Look at this drawing of the fire god Agni. By darkening the space behind him, you create a rounded, three-dimensional effect. You can imagine Agni illuminating the night sky as he flies from place to place spreading light and warmth. Adding shading to the fire god also contributes to the rounded, three-dimensional look.

58

MAKING YOUR CHARACTER SEEM LARGER (OR SMALLER)

How do you make a figure in a small drawing appear larger? Or a character in a huge picture seem smaller? The following techniques will show you how.

THE HORIZON LINE AND ADDING OBJECTS FOR SCALE

To show how big your character is in a drawing, add a ground line or a horizon line across your picture. Normally, the horizon line is at the viewer's eye level. So, if you draw the top of your figure higher than the horizon line, it seems larger. If you draw the horizon line near the top of your picture and place your character toward the bottom, the character seems smaller. Look at this picture of Jormungand, the Midgard serpent. The top of the serpent is drawn above the horizon line—which, in this case, is the line depicting the curve of the earth. This placement makes the serpent look very large, as big as the earth itself.

Another way to indicate a character's size is to include in your drawing objects whose size most people know. For example, people know that the earth's continents are very large. Therefore, drawing partial outlines of the continents next to the serpent also helps to emphasize the serpent's immense size.

TIPS ON COLOR

Your picture will stand out from the rest of the crowd if you use these helpful tips on how to add color to your masterpiece!

TRY WHITE ON BLACK

For a different look, try working on black construction paper or art paper. Then, instead of pencil, use white chalk, white prismacolor, or poster paint. With this technique, you'll need to concentrate on drawing the light areas in your picture rather than the dark ones. This technique is great for drawing the jinni because it accentuates the texture of the smoke surrounding its body.

TRY BLACK AND WHITE ON TAN (OR GRAY)

You don't need special tan or gray paper from the art store for this technique. Instead, try cutting apart the inside of a grocery bag or a cereal box. This time, your background is a middle tone (neither light nor dark). Sketch your character in black, then use white to make highlights. Add black for shadows. Don't completely cover up the tan or gray on the cardboard. Let it be the middle tone within your illustration. With this technique, your pictures can have a very finished look with a minimal amount of drawing.

TRY COLOR

Instead of using every color in your marker, colored pencil, or paint set, try rendering in black for shadows, white for highlights, and one color for a middle tone. This third color blended with the white creates a fourth color. You will be surprised how professional your drawing will look.

61

GLOSSARY

Aladdin: one of the characters in *A Thousand and One Nights*. He comes into possession of a magic lamp that houses a jinni who grants him three wishes.

Asclepius: Greek god of medicine and the son of Apollo. He is raised by Chiron to be a great healer. Zeus kills Asclepius with a thunderbolt because the god feels Asclepius's ability to revive the dead threatens the natural order of the world.

Athena: Greek goddess of wisdom (Roman goddess Minerva). She sprang to life from Zeus's head, fully grown and dressed in a complete suit of armor. The Greek city of Athens was named after her.

Cupid: Roman god of love (Greek god Eros). The son of Venus and Mars, he makes people fall in love by shooting magic arrows at them.

Daedalus: craftsman in Greek mythology who builds the labyrinth that houses the Minotaur. After Theseus slays the Minotaur and escapes from the labyrinth, King Minos punishes Daedalus by placing him and his son, Icarus, in jail. The two escape when Daedalus designs wings of wax and feathers for himself and his son. As they are flying away, Icarus flies too close to the sun and falls to his death.

Dis: Roman god of the underworld (Greek god Hades, or Pluto) and Jupiter's brother. He lends the young hero Perseus his winged sandals when he goes to slay the Gorgon Medusa.

Excalibur: King Arthur's magic sword. After he is mortally wounded by Mordred, Arthur asks one of his knights to throw the sword into the lake, then return and tell Arthur what he saw. The knight reports that the water formed into the shape of a hand that reached up out of the water and caught the sword.

fairy tale: a make-believe story about fairies, wizards, giants, or other characters who possess magical or unusual powers

folklore: traditions, customs, and stories of one culture or group of people

Freya: Norse goddess of love, fertility, and beauty. This beautiful goddess usually travels in a chariot drawn by cats.

Gorgon: any of the three Greek sisters—Stheno, Euryale, and Medusa—who have snakes for hair. Anyone who looks directly at a Gorgon immediately turns to stone.

Huginn: one of Odin's ravens. Its name means "thought."

immortal: able to live forever; exempt from death

Jason: Greek mythological hero. As the son of the Greek king Aeson, he is famous for retrieving the Golden Fleece from the evil King Aeëtes.

Jupiter: the king of the Roman gods (Greek god Zeus). He is married to the goddess Juno but has many other romances with goddesses and mortal women. He is the father of many children.

legend: a story about the past that is considered to be true but is usually a combination of both fact and fiction

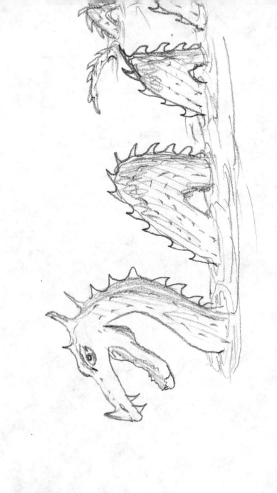

Dear Grammy & Grandpa

Loki: Norse god known as the trickster. The embodiment of evil among the Norse gods, he is the father of the Fenrir wolf and the Midgard serpent.

Mars: Roman god of war (Greek god Ares). He falls in love with Venus, and the two of them have a son, Cupid, the god of love. Mars is known for his fierce temper.

Merlin: King Arthur's adviser and wizard. After serving Arthur for many years, Merlin falls in love with a cruel fairy who imprisons him inside a magical forest.

Middle Ages: period in Europe from the fifth to the fifteenth centuries

Minerva: Roman goddess of wisdom; see Athena

Minos: king of the Greek city Crete and Zeus's son. After King Minos dies, he becomes a judge of the dead in the underworld.

Mordred: King Arthur's son and most bitter enemy. Mordred wages war on Arthur in an attempt to take over the throne of Britain.

Mount Olympus: home of the Greek gods, located in the region of Greece called Thessaly. Though most of the gods reside here—ruled by Zeus—they roam freely about the earth.

Muninn: one of Odin's ravens. Its name means "memory."

myth: a story that explains the beliefs, practices, and rituals of a culture

mythology: a group of myths from a single group or culture

Neptune: Roman god of the sea (Greek god Poseidon). He has the ability to stir up and calm the ocean waters.

oracle: a person through whom a god or goddess supposedly speaks. Oracles can often foresee the future and are common figures in Greek and Roman mythology.

Pegasus: the winged horse who comes to life from the Gorgon Medusa's decapitated body

Poseidon: Greek god of the sea; see Neptune

Python: Greek serpent whom Apollo slays. The Python came to life out of the slime left on earth after a huge flood. Its mother is said to be Gaea, the goddess of the earth.

supernatural: more than what is natural or normal; showing godlike or magical powers; exhibiting superhuman strength

Tezcatlipoca: Toltec god of the night sky, the moon, and the stars. He is associated with evil forces and is a master of black magic.

A Thousand and One Nights (**also known as** *The Arabian Nights*): a collection of stories and fables from Arabia, Egypt, India, and Persia that were compiled from oral tales that had been passed down through these cultures for generations. Some of the more well-known characters include Aladdin, Ali Baba, and Sinbad the Sailor. Jinn are common figures in these stories.

Through the Looking Glass: a fictional story by Lewis Carroll published in 1872. It tells about the adventures of a young girl named Alice in a world behind a mirror.

Vulcan: Roman god of fire (Greek god Hephaestus). The son of Jupiter and Juno, his leg is injured when he is thrown from Mount Olympus during an argument his parents are having.

Zeus: king of the Greek gods; see Jupiter

THE GREEK AND ROMAN GODS

The Greek culture existed before the Roman culture. When the Romans decided to develop a mythology, they adopted the gods of Greek mythology and changed their names. Typically, these Roman versions of the gods are more disciplined and do not take on the same colorful and complex personalities that many of the Greek gods have. Following is a list of equivalent Greek and Roman gods.

GREEK	ROMAN	TITLE
Aphrodite	Venus	goddess of love and beauty
Apollo	Apollo	god of music, poetry, and the sun
Ares	Mars	god of war
Artemis	Diana	goddess of the moon
Asclepius	Aesculapius	god of medicine
Athena	Minerva	goddess of wisdom
Cronus	Saturn	god of the sky and agriculture
Eros	Cupid	god of love
Gaea	Terra	Mother Earth
Hades	Dis	god of the underworld
Hephaestus	Vulcan	god of fire; craftsman for the gods
Hera	Juno	queen of the gods; goddess of marriage
Hermes	Mercury	messenger of the gods
Poseidon	Neptune	god of the sea
Zeus	Jupiter	ruler of the gods